The *ultimate* source for Blues Riffs & Licks

great **Riffs** series

Blues Riffs

for Piano

by Ed Baker

PLAYBACK+

Speed • Pitch • Balance • Loop

To access audio visit:
www.halleonard.com/mylibrary

Enter Code
4244-2472-3281-5984

ISBN 978-0-89524-929-6

ᵀᴹ cherry lane
music company

EXCLUSIVELY DISTRIBUTED BY

HAL•LEONARD®

7777 W. BLUEMOUND RD. P.O. BOX 13819 MILWAUKEE, WI 53213

Visit Hal Leonard Online at
www.halleonard.com

About The Author

Fred Dobro

Ed Baker has worked as a composer, arranger and keyboardist for various documentaries, jingles and Off-Broadway shows. A former member of the NightTrain Blues Band and the Smokin' EE's, he works as a freelance musician in New York City. In addition to being a published songwriter, film credits include composing an original score for the film *Mixed Signals*, and co-writing "Some People Say," the theme song from the movie *Let It Be Me*. He is a staff teacher and creator of the blues piano curriculum at the Guitar Study Center at the New School For Social Research in New York City.

∽ Acknowledgments ∽

Putting a book together is a group effort, and I would like to thank the following: Jon Chappell for all his help and guidance; all the folks at Cherry Lane Music for their support; Frank Pekoc for a great engineering job and his unlimited patience; Jonathan Perl for his MIDI magic; and City College for the use of their recording facilities. And, finally, to all the blues masters I've listened to, learned from and enjoyed throughout the years.

Thank you all!

E. B.

HOW TO USE THIS BOOK

THIS BOOK is *not* progressive in that the riffs are not presented in order of increasing difficulty. Instead they are grouped by their function in a musical setting: comping patterns, fills, turn-arounds, etc. You should therefore proceed according to interest and necessity.

Practice each hand separately at a manageable tempo before putting both hands together. Sound like your old music lessons? It should—it works!

Work these riffs out in various keys. Eventually you should learn these riffs in all keys, but be practical and start with C, F, Bb, G, and then the "guitar" keys: E, A, D, G, and C. Those of you who play an electronic keyboard should by all means resist the temptation to transpose digitally—it will catch you red-faced someday.

The riffs in this volume are presented the way *I play them*, which is neither the correct nor the only way of doing so. You will see and hear occasions where the transcription is not exact, due to subtleties in the performance that could not be notated except by unnecessarily complex notation. In these instances you should play both what you hear and what you see. In *all* instances you should push, pull, and generally massage the notes until you arrive at that point where the riff becomes your own—recognizably blues yet unique to your style.

If blues music is not a passion for you the reader, the ability to play even the basics is most certainly a skill every well-rounded pop pianist should have in his repertoire. In fact, the "cross pollenization" of blues music with other styles is so evident in contemporary music that many of the riffs presented in this volume will play just as well in a jazz, country, or a rock setting, requiring nothing more than an "attitude" adjustment from the player.

EDITOR'S NOTE: Much of the music in this book is played in a triplet feel, where two eighth notes starting on a downbeat equal . In instances where triplets and eighth notes appear simultaneously, as when the right hand plays three triplet eighths against the left hand's two eighths, it is the third triplet of the right hand that coincides with the left hand's second eighth note.

CONTENTS

ROOTS

Blues has its origins in the African music that the first slaves transplanted to the southern United States, where each tribal group steadfastly retained its own linguistic and musical traditions. Though, as a musical form, blues did not exist during the more than 200 years of American slavery, during this time there was a blending of innumerable kinds of music. Black musicians were playing everything from purely African music to purely white American music. Despite the borrowing that went on musically between the races, the black performing style remained distinctive, with black songsters developing a body of music radically different from the white and interracial common stock. It wasn't until the 1890s that blues developed as a musical genre.

THE BLUES NOTES

Blues was heavily influenced by field hollers and work songs. These melodies sound like they are based on the major scale with the flattening in pitch around the 3rd, 5th and 7th. The flatted 3rd is the expressive core of the hollers, work songs, spirituals and, later, the blues. Blues became a more formalized music than hollers and work songs in the late 19th century, with a tendency toward 12-bar, AAA- or AAB-verse forms, or pentatonic melodies with a flatted 3rd.

SOUTHERN DIVERSITY

Early southeastern blues was more of a ballad or ragtime nature, while in east Texas the guitar-accompanied blues tended to be rhythmically diffuse with elaborate melodic flourishes to answer vocal lines. At the same time, a black piano tradition that emphasized driving dance rhythms was materializing in the lumber and turpentine camps of Texas and Louisiana. Veterans of these work camps and barrelhouses were Memphis Slim, Jack Dupree, Little Brother Montgomery, Roosevelt Sykes, Sunnyland Slim and Speckled Red.

THE RHYTHMIC ELEMENT

The blues piano tradition really began as a mocking of railroad train sounds—a rhythmic bass with the intent of capturing the pattern of rail clicks was one of the first things all players learned as children. The pianist's job was to keep the people dancing; boogie-woogie probably developed out of this kind of playing, transforming the piano into a polyrhythmic railroad train. The left hand hammered out eight insistent beats to the bar while the right hand played melodies that were essentially rhythmic variations on the bass line. As dance halls grew bigger, pianos and small combos began replacing the lone guitarist, as boogie-woogie on the upright—with the front out and buzzers on the strings—could reach to the back tables in a big, noisy barroom.

URBAN BLUES

As the piano, an orchestra in miniature, can also be a drum, Delta blues piano accompaniments were more percussive and hypnotic than boogie-woogie; here, "crushing the ivories" far superseded "tickling the ivories." The black migration northward at the end of the century helped spread this new style to the cities, and players like Otis Spann, Sunnyland Slim and Memphis Slim brought their Delta blues piano style to Chicago.

THE MODERN BLUES ERA

Blues piano exploded during the Second World War years. In the 1940s "jump blues" was the rage, with innovators such as jazz legend Count Basie leading the way. In New Orleans, Professor Longhair was introducing Latin and rhumba figures, full of polyrhythms, to his basic blues piano. He is considered the "Father of New Orleans R & B," and his influence can be heard in the music of Dr. John and Allen Toussaint, among others. In St. Louis during the 1950s, Johnny Johnson played a crucial part in Chuck Berry's pioneering rock 'n' roll sound, and continues to record and perform his St. Louis-style blues today. Ray Charles, another star of the blues firmament in the '50s and '60s, fused gospel and blues to create a style that has influenced all modern soul music. Regardless of style, it is nearly impossible to listen to contemporary pianists and not hear the profound influence of the blues legacy.

INTRODUCTION

Following is a musical outline or map of the 12-bar blues. Most of the licks, comping figures, turnarounds and tags will fit comfortably in this framework. Whenever you play the blues, it is essential to always know where you are in the arrangement.

12-Bar Blues

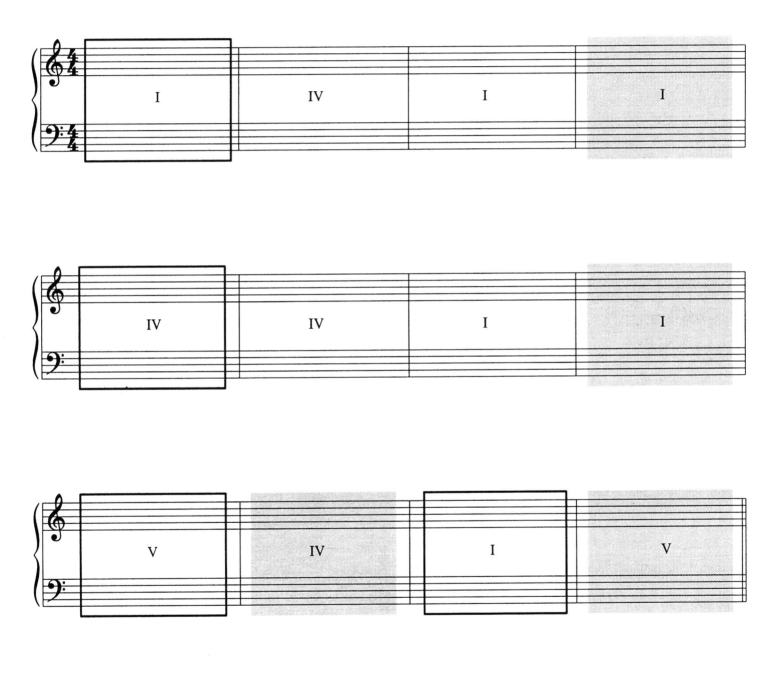

STRUCTURE This is one of the most common arrangements of a 12-bar blues. The boxed measures indicate the structure. All chords include the minor 7ths. In the key of C, the chords are C7, F7, and G7.

FILLS The measures shaded in are where the fills go. By definition, a fill is a change of texture. On the piano, we have several ways of changing the texture: a right-hand melodic lick, left-hand bass line, rhythmic change between the left and right hand, changing octaves, and any combination of the above. The biggest fill occurs in measure 10.

The Pentatonic Scale

The pentatonic scale is used extensively in the blues. This is a five-tone scale that is comprised of scale steps 1, 2, 3, 5 and 6 from the diatonic major scale. Passing tones are added between scale steps 2-3, and 5-6.

Pentatonic Exercise

Pentatonic exercise is one way of grouping the notes of the scale for solos and fills. Included are two variations of the exercise; Variation #2 includes the two passing tones. Slide the third finger—do not pull your hand.

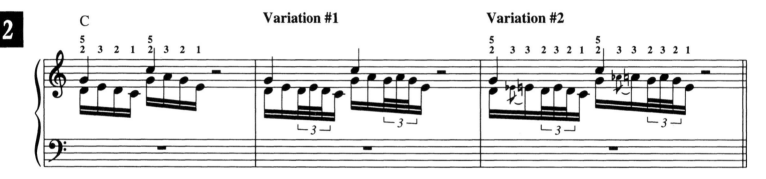

Suspensions

Suspensions are a common way to create movement without going anywhere, and are a great way of killing time while playing one chord. The different suspensions include the sus4, sus2, sus4/sus2, and the full suspension, which is the same as the 2nd-inversion IV chord.

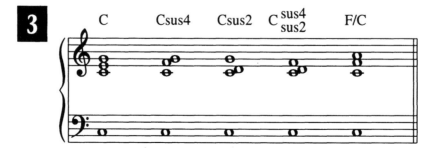

12-Bar Blues

This is a common arrangement of a 12-bar blues. Note how the chord voicing is split between the two hands; movement is between the inner voices. This should be practiced with both a triplet- and eighth-note feel. The second and fourth chord in every measure is a full suspension. Bar 1: C, F/C, C7, F/C.

Sliding Notes And Crushing Notes

Sliding notes and crushing notes allow the piano player to get to the flatted 3rds and flatted 5ths, which are an integral part of the blues sound. Make sure that the grace note being crushed is released while holding the other note. Slides and crushes can be played at various speeds.

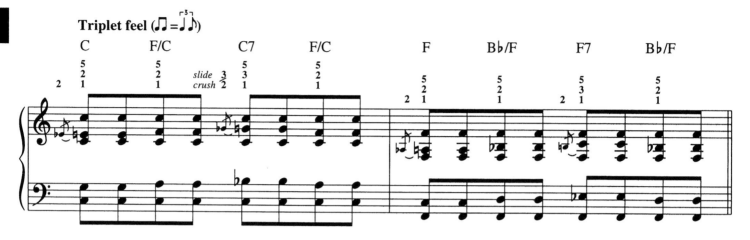

Now incorporate the ♭3rd and ♭5th into the previous example. Sometimes you have the option of sliding or crushing the ♭5th. Slides and crushes produce different phrasing. Try both, and practice this in all keys.

Neighbor Chords

Another common way to create movement while comping is to approach chords from both a half-step above and a half-step below. Suspended chords also work well here as they add to the movement.

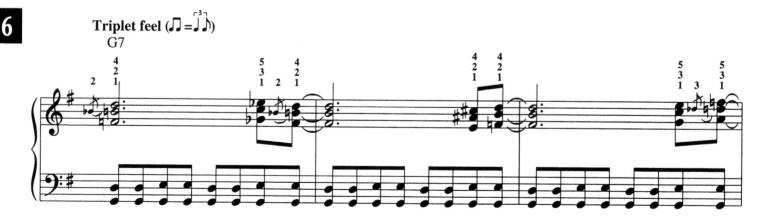

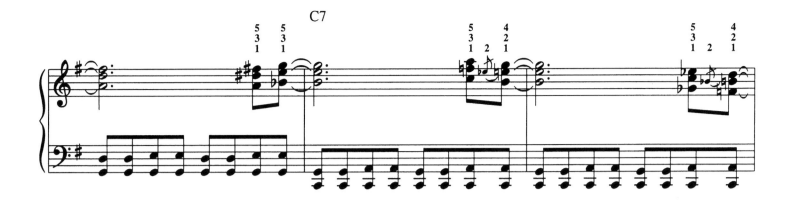

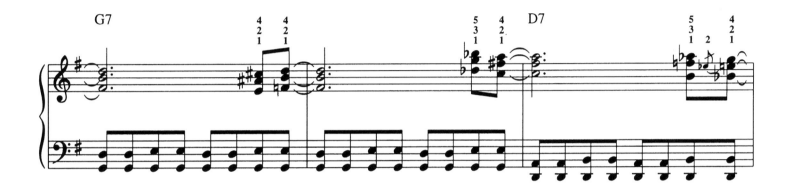

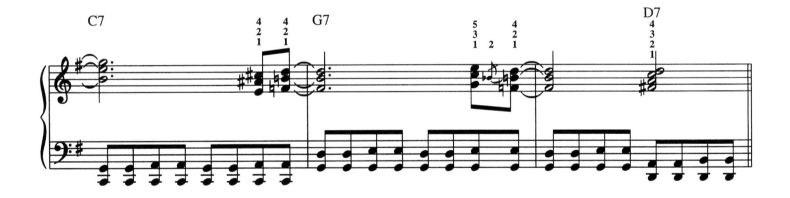

Altered Notes

Here is a common use of the flatted 3rd, flatted 5th, 7th and the full suspension (Db/Ab). Make sure you hold the quarter note in the right hand for the full beat. Check the fingering!

Running Triplets

This is a variation of #7. It gets you to play two different phrases in your right hand at the same time. Instead of anchoring your hand down with one finger holding the quarter note, you must slide the bottom note while repeating the top note.

D

G

Jimmy Yancey–Type Parallel 3rds

Jimmy Yancey, a well known Chicago pianist, plays this well-known riff using the flatted 3rd, flatted 5th and the full suspension (F/C). Notice the movement of parallel 3rds.

9

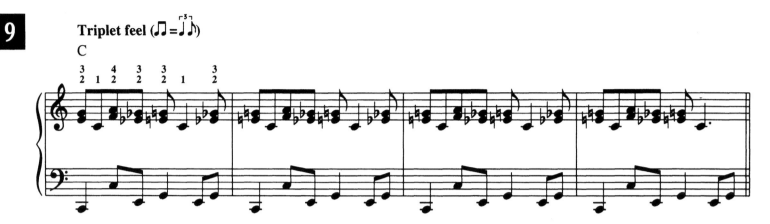

Jimmy Yancey–Type Parallel 6ths

Here is a variation of the previous figure. Inverting the parallel 3rds creates parallel 6ths. The 4th connects the 5th and the 3rd.

10

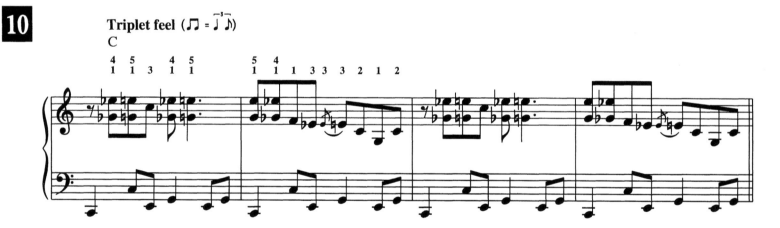

Jimmy Yancey–Type Boogie

This is the kind of early boogie-woogie Jimmy Yancey would play. It employs great use of the flat 3rd and flat 5th sliding as parallel 3rds to the 3rd and 5th. To create a solo, start with a simple riff and repeat it, building as you go along. This is the same left-hand part that Professor Longhair used for his hit song "Tipitina."

11

Boogie-Woogie Walking Bass

Another variation is to play the octave. This is the kind of riff you hear Dr. John play over the I chord. Count straight 16ths.

12

Huey Smith–Type Riff

This lick is the kind of figure Professor Longhair and Huey Smith played a lot. A and B are variations of the original riff. Notice the different ways the beat is being split up. Count straight eighths.

13

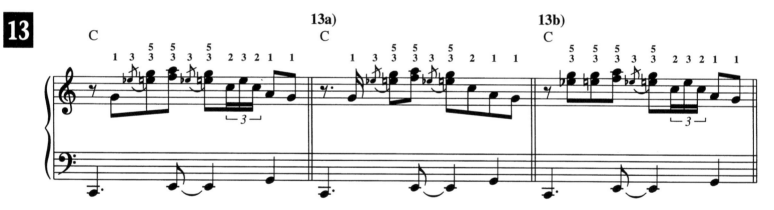

Ostinato Riff

This use of the flatted 3rd is common—no slide here. This line sounds great whether played over the I, IV, or V chord. Check out how the sus4, sus4/sus2 creates movement at the end of beats 1 and 3. Notice the voicing of the sus4/sus2.

14

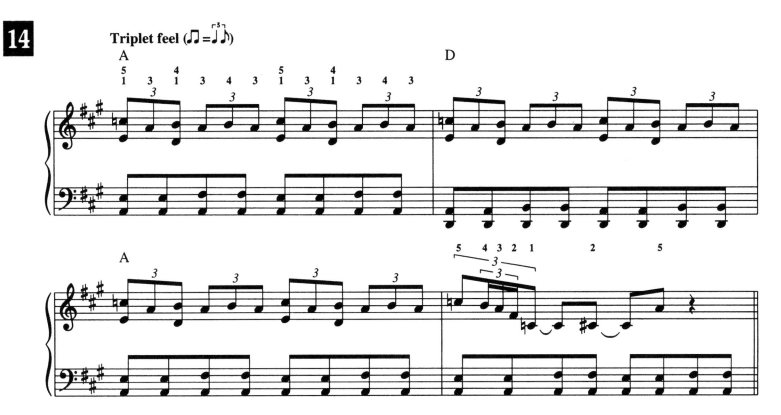

Texas Boogie–Type Riff

Johnny Johnson and Dr. John use this riff often. The harmonic movement is C9, F/C, C7. This works well for both soloing and comping.

15

I To V

Here is a funky New Orleans riff that works well at the end of an 8- or 12- bar structure going from the I to the V chord. Check out the movement of the bass line.

Ray Charles–Type Riff

Ray Charles makes great use of the pentatonic scale here. Both passing tones are being used. The chromatic bass line can be heard in Charles' early recordings. This lick works over the I, IV, and V chords, although it makes for a strong line leading from the IV chord to the I chord.

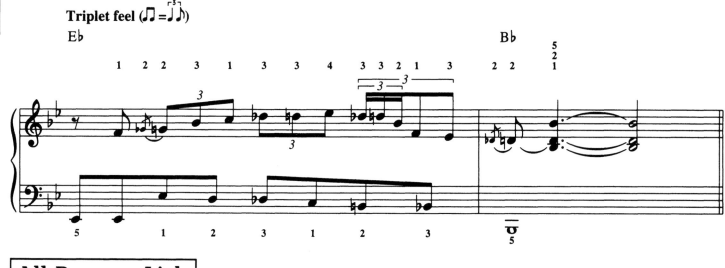

All-Purpose Lick

It is hard to say where this lick originated, but it is used by everyone and heard often. There are modifications of it throughout this book.

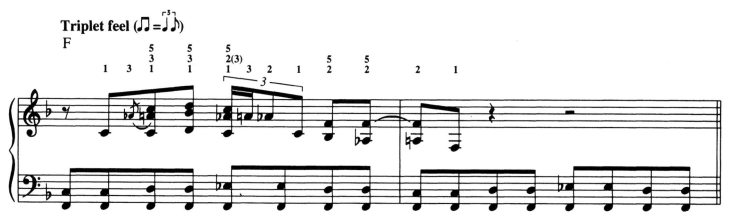

All Purpose Variation #1

Here is a variation of the previous lick that you may also hear Ray Charles play. Check out how the bass line harmonizes with the flat 5 and the 4th.

19

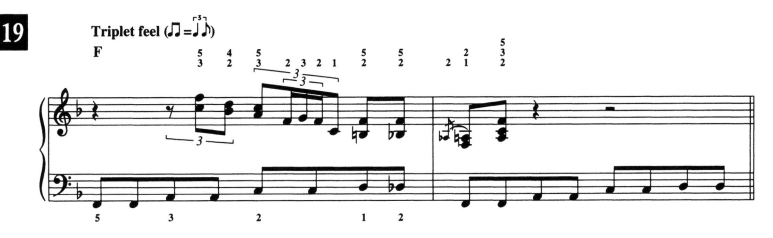

All Purpose Variation #2

This is a variation of the previous example, and is one more way Charles makes use of the pentatonic scale and full suspensions.

20

Bar-Line Break-Up

Notice how this phrase goes through the bar line; you do not feel the downbeat in the right hand. Roll the notes after you have learned the lick. This is the kind of line Johnny Johnson likes to play.

21

Turnaround #1

This is an often-used turnaround. Check the harmonic walk-up to the V chord. Augmenting the V chord (raising the 5th a half step) is common and works great in ballads and introductions.

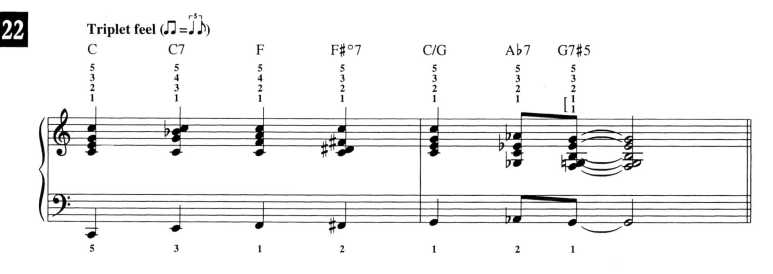

Turnaround #2

Here is a variation of the previous turnaround. Willie Tee favors this version, which has more of a New Orleans feel to it.

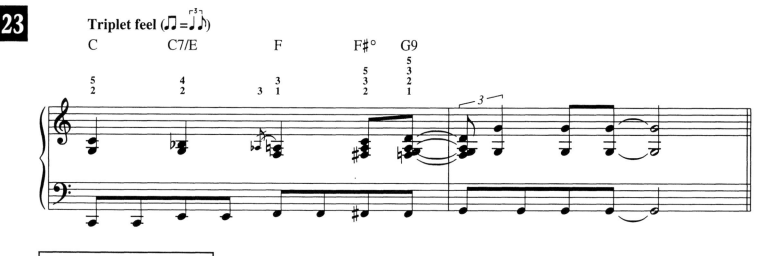

Turnaround #3

Below is another common turnaround: parallel 3rds walking down in the right hand while the left hand walks chromatically. All this movement is driving you to the I chord. The top note is a constant C.

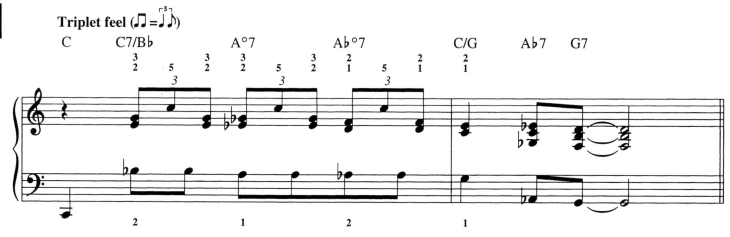

Pentatonic Turnaround #1

Dr. John is one of many New Orleans artists that uses this pentatonic turnaround. It is played with a straight eighth-note feel. Notice how the bass line walks you from the V chord to the I chord and back down to the V chord. The last measure has a nice New Orleans syncopated feel.

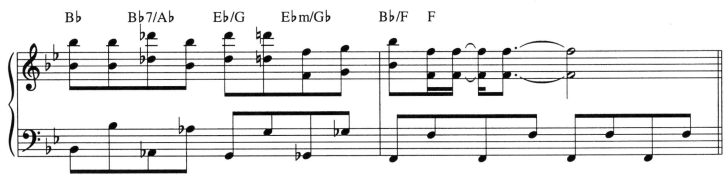

Pentatonic Turnaround #2

This is the kind of variation Otis Spann would play on the previous turnaround.

Tag #1

This is a revoicing of Example 24. You now have parallel 6ths moving down, and the movement in the right hand is the reverse of Example 24 with the bottom note being a constant C.

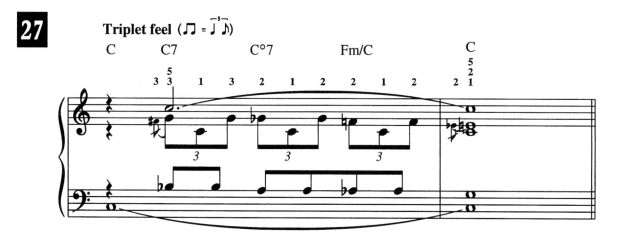

I-IV Walk-Up #1

Here is a common New Orleans walk-up to the IV chord. Professor Longhair made use of this lick, and his protégé, Dr. John, among others, continues to use it as well. Even though you are playing straight 16ths, the phrasing here is in three's.

I-IV Walk-Up #2

'Fess liked to use this lick as well; it's a variation of the one above. The lick is broken up between the two hands, and you should feel more weight at the beginning of every three notes. Sounds great with a very syncopated feel.

Willie Tee–Type IV Approach

Willie Tee likes to approach the IV chord this way. Notice the chromatic chord on beat 2. This is similar to #7—approaching chords from a half step above and below.

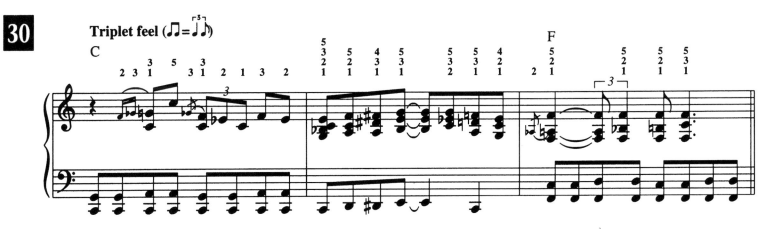

IV Intro Walk-Up

Here is another common riff that is used as a walk-up to the IV chord, an introduction, and a solo. Ray Charles, Dr. John, and countless others use this riff. These notes are specific to the chord you are playing—in this case a C7.

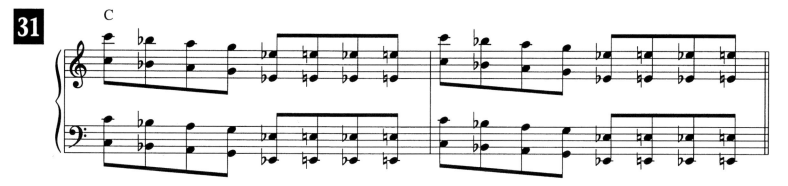

Rolling Notes

Rolling notes, particularly 3rds, 6ths, octaves and 9ths, is a common way of ornamenting a lick. Here, I'm rolling 3rds and moving in parallel 3rds walking to and from all the chords. This technique imitates the tremolo of a stringed instrument.

Crushing And Sliding #1

This common blues riff is based around the flat 5. The top note is the 7th, which contributes to the intensity of the sound. This makes use of crushes and slides.

33

Crushing And Sliding #2

This is a variation of the above riff and uses only the notes from the blues scale (1 ♭3 4 ♭5 5 ♭7).

34

Stride Lick In 10ths

In this example, the left hand is playing 10ths in a stride style. The right hand is walking chromatically to the IV chord and switching to an F pentatonic scale over the IV chord. You can open up your solo by changing scales as the chords change.

35

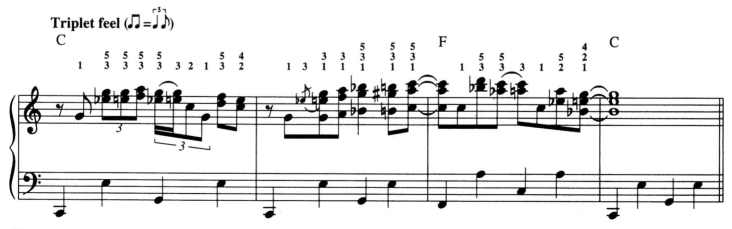

Left-Hand 10ths

Again, you are playing 10ths with the left hand. This time the 10ths are played together, and works well for slower tempos. The right hand plays straight pentatonic; beat 3 in measure 1 is a common pentatonic riff. Watch your fingering.

36

V-Chord Lick

A common use of this lick over the V chord. Allen Toussaint and Katie Webster use this kind of riff as both an intro and an approach to the turnaround.

37

Full-Length 16-Bar Swing Solo

This full-length solo begins and ends with two different tags. Check how the bass line moves from a pattern to a walking line to 10ths. Your left hand should be independent enough to move the part around. The walk-up in bar 8 works well as a fill by changing the texture.

38

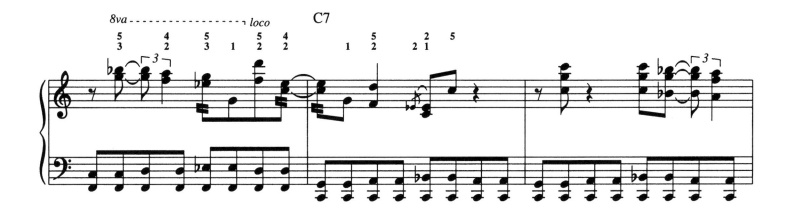

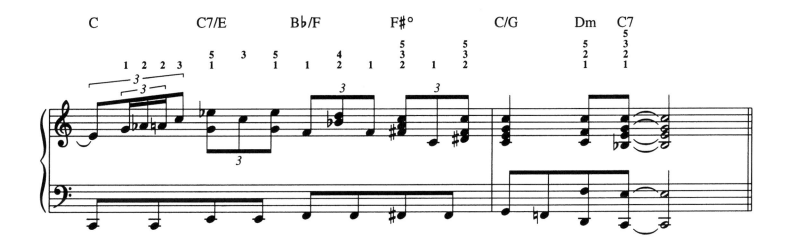

12-Bar Cow Cow Boogie-Woogie Variation

Here you have a full-length solo with an 8th-note feel, reminiscent of the "Cow-Cow Boogie," originated by Cow-Cow Davenport. The harmonic structure is a little different. The fill in bar 4 uses rhythm to change the texture, and employs suspensions for movement. I also switch to the F pentatonic scale (F G A C D) when playing the IV chord—to open up the solo—before returning to C pentatonic (C D E G A). Notice how some of these riffs basically outline the chord being played.

39

KEYBOARD STYLE SERIES

THE COMPLETE GUIDE!

These book/audio packs provide focused lessons that contain valuable how-to insight, essential playing tips, and beneficial information for all players. From comping to soloing, comprehensive treatment is given to each subject. The companion audio features many of the examples in the book performed either solo or with a full band.

BEBOP JAZZ PIANO
by John Valerio

This book provides detailed information for bebop and jazz keyboardists on: chords and voicings, harmony and chord progressions, scales and tonality, common melodic figures and patterns, comping, characteristic tunes, the styles of Bud Powell and Thelonious Monk, and more.

00290535 Book/Online Audio $18.99

BEGINNING ROCK KEYBOARD
by Mark Harrison

This comprehensive book/audio package will teach you the basic skills needed to play beginning rock keyboard. From comping to soloing, you'll learn the theory, the tools, and the techniques used by the pros. The accompanying audio demonstrates most of the music examples in the book.

00311922 Book/Online Audio $14.99

BLUES PIANO
by Mark Harrison

With this book/audio pack, you'll learn the theory, the tools, and even the tricks that the pros use to play the blues. Covers: scales and chords; left-hand patterns; walking bass; endings and turnarounds; right-hand techniques; how to solo with blues scales; crossover licks; and more.

00311007 Book/Online Audio $19.99

BOOGIE-WOOGIE PIANO
by Todd Lowry

From learning the basic chord progressions to inventing your own melodic riffs, you'll learn the theory, tools and techniques used by the genre's best practicioners.

00117067 Book/Online Audio $17.99

BRAZILIAN PIANO
by Robert Willey and Alfredo Cardim

Brazilian Piano teaches elements of some of the most appealing Brazilian musical styles: choro, samba, and bossa nova. It starts with rhythmic training to develop the fundamental groove of Brazilian music.

00311469 Book/Online Audio $19.99

CONTEMPORARY JAZZ PIANO
by Mark Harrison

From comping to soloing, you'll learn the theory, the tools, and the techniques used by the pros. The full band tracks on the audio feature the rhythm section on the left channel and the piano on the right channel, so that you can play along with the band.

00311848 Book/Online Audio $18.99

COUNTRY PIANO
by Mark Harrison

Learn the theory, the tools, and the tricks used by the pros to get that authentic country sound. This book/audio pack covers: scales and chords, walkup and walkdown patterns, comping in traditional and modern country, Nashville "fretted piano" techniques and more.

00311052 Book/Online Audio $19.99

GOSPEL PIANO
by Kurt Cowling

Discover the tools you need to play in a variety of authentic gospel styles, through a study of rhythmic devices, grooves, melodic and harmonic techniques, and formal design. The accompanying audio features over 90 tracks, including piano examples as well as the full gospel band.

00311327 Book/Online Adio $17.99

INTRO TO JAZZ PIANO
by Mark Harrison

From comping to soloing, you'll learn the theory, the tools, and the techniques used by the pros. The accompanying audio demonstrates most of the music examples in the book. The full band tracks feature the rhythm section on the left channel and the piano on the right channel, so that you can play along with the band.

00312088 Book/Online Audio $17.99

JAZZ-BLUES PIANO
by Mark Harrison

This comprehensive book will teach you the basic skills needed to play jazz-blues piano. Topics covered include: scales and chords • harmony and voicings • progressions and comping • melodies and soloing • characteristic stylings.

00311243 Book/Online Audio $17.99

JAZZ-ROCK KEYBOARD
by T. Lavitz

Learn what goes into mixing the power and drive of rock music with the artistic elements of jazz improvisation in this comprehensive book and CD package. This instructional tool delves into scales and modes, and how they can be used with various chord progressions to develop the best in soloing chops.

00290536 Book/CD Pack $17.95

LATIN JAZZ PIANO
by John Valerio

This book is divided into three sections. The first covers Afro-Cuban (Afro-Caribbean) jazz, the second section deals with Brazilian influenced jazz – Bossa Nova and Samba, and the third contains lead sheets of the tunes and instructions for the play-along audio.

00311345 Book/Online Audio $17.99

MODERN POP KEYBOARD
by Mark Harrison

From chordal comping to arpeggios and ostinatos, from grand piano to synth pads, you'll learn the theory, the tools, and the techniques used by the pros. The online audio demonstrates most of the music examples in the book.

00146596 Book/Online Audio $17.99

NEW AGE PIANO
by Todd Lowry

From melodic development to chord progressions to left-hand accompaniment patterns, you'll learn the theory, the tools and the techniques used by the pros. The accompanying 96-track CD demonstrates most of the music examples in the book.

00117322 Book/CD Pack $16.99

POST-BOP JAZZ PIANO
by John Valerio

This book/audio pack will teach you the basic skills needed to play post-bop jazz piano. Learn the theory, the tools, and the tricks used by the pros to play in the style of Bill Evans, Thelonious Monk, Herbie Hancock, McCoy Tyner, Chick Corea and others. Topics covered include: chord voicings, scales and tonality, modality, and more.

00311005 Book/Online Audio $17.99

PROGRESSIVE ROCK KEYBOARD
by Dan Maske

You'll learn how soloing techniques, form, rhythmic and metrical devices, harmony, and counterpoint all come together to make this style of rock the unique and exciting genre it is.

00311307 Book/Online Audio $19.99

R&B KEYBOARD
by Mark Harrison

From soul to funk to disco to pop, you'll learn the theory, the tools, and the tricks used by the pros with this book/audio pack. Topics covered include: scales and chords, harmony and voicings, progressions and comping, rhythmic concepts, characteristic stylings, the development of R&B, and more! Includes seven songs.

00310881 Book/Online Audio $19.99

ROCK KEYBOARD
by Scott Miller

Learn to comp or solo in any of your favorite rock styles. Listen to the audio to hear your parts fit in with the total groove of the band. Includes 99 tracks! Covers: classic rock, pop/rock, blues rock, Southern rock, hard rock, progressive rock, alternative rock and heavy metal.

00310823 Book/Online Audio $17.99

ROCK 'N' ROLL PIANO
by Andy Vinter

Take your place alongside Fats Domino, Jerry Lee Lewis, Little Richard, and other legendary players of the '50s and '60s! This book/audio pack covers: left-hand patterns; basic rock 'n' roll progressions; right-hand techniques; straight eighths vs. swing eighths; glisses; crushed notes, rolls, note clusters and more. Includes six complete tunes.

00310912 Book/Online Audio $18.99

SALSA PIANO
by Hector Martignon

From traditional Cuban music to the more modern Puerto Rican and New York styles, you'll learn the all-important rhythmic patterns of salsa and how to apply them to the piano. The book provides historical, geographical and cultural background info, and the 50+-tracks includes piano examples and a full salsa band percussion section.

00311049 Book/Online Audio $19.99

SMOOTH JAZZ PIANO
by Mark Harrison

Learn the skills you need to play smooth jazz piano – the theory, the tools, and the tricks used by the pros. Topics covered include: scales and chords; harmony and voicings; progressions and comping; rhythmic concepts; melodies and soloing; characteristic stylings; discussions on jazz evolution.

00311095 Book/Online Audio $19.99

STRIDE & SWING PIANO
by John Valerio

Learn the styles of the stride and swing piano masters, such as Scott Joplin, Jimmy Yancey, Pete Johnson, Jelly Roll Morton, James P. Johnson, Fats Waller, Teddy Wilson, and Art Tatum. This book/audio pack covers classic ragtime, early blues and boogie woogie, New Orleans jazz and more. Includes 14 songs.

00310882 Book/Online Audio $19.99

WORSHIP PIANO
by Bob Kauflin

From chord inversions to color tones, from rhythmic patterns to the Nashville Numbering System, you'll learn the tools and techniques needed to play piano or keyboard in a modern worship setting.

00311425 Book/Online Audio $17.99

HAL•LEONARD®

Prices, contents, and availability
subject to change without notice.

www.halleonard.com